assisted by Martyn Rix
Jacqui Hurst and Nicky Foy

Elm Tree Books London

INTRODUCTION

Aim

In this book we have aimed to photograph and describe 92 of the native or commonly planted trees of the British Isles and northern Europe, together with several rare and interesting ones.

How to use this book

The trees are arranged according to their leaf shapes, beginning with the conifers with scale-like leaves, followed by conifers with short needles, then those such as pines, with long needles. The broad-leaved trees begin with those with narrow, simple leaves, followed by those with broader leaves, wavy-edged or lobed leaves, and ending with compound leaves such as the Horse Chestnut, and pinnate leaves such as ash and walnut.

In most cases one photograph shows the leaves and flowers of the tree so that all the relevant details can be clearly seen, the other shows the tree growing, to give an idea of its shape, the angle of its branches and density of its leaves and, where applicable, flowers.

What is a native tree?

At the height of the last ice age, as little as 20,000 years ago, there were probably no full sized trees in the British Isles, at least north of a line from London to Bristol. As the climate became warmer in about 9,000 BC, the tree belts migrated northwards from southern Europe, first birches and conifers, such as Scots Pine; later broad-leaved deciduous trees such as oaks reached this country, pushing the pines north to Scotland and covering with forest most of the lowlands. Not many different trees had reached Britain before the Channel was formed by rising sea level, and

further migration from the Continent ceased. Of the trees shown in this book, only 30 or so are considered truly native. Others, such as ash, may have been encouraged by Neolithic man as he cleared the original forests, and others which may appear wild such as the Sweet and Horse Chestnuts were certainly introduced in historical time, the former probably by the Romans, the latter in the early 17th century.

Help protect our remaining woodlands
The primaeval woodlands which formerly covered most of the British Isles have long gone but many old woods still survive, either more or less natural or else planted hundreds of years ago, and it is there that the best native trees and woodland flowers can be found. Once woods have been rooted up, they can never be replaced, as even if the trees are replanted, the wild flowers and animals take hundreds of years to recolonize them.

In the last fifty years many areas of woodland have been totally lost but recently the destruction has slowed. Many have been saved by being necessary for the maintenance of pheasant shoots; others have been saved by law or by being bought or given to national bodies such as the Woodland Trust.

The Photographs
The studio photographs were taken on a Bronica 120 format with a 75mm lens. Scale: ○ is 1cm. The field photographs were taken on a Nikon FM camera with a 50mm lens, occasionally with close-up attachments. The film was Kodak Ektachrome 64 ASA in both cases, but when used outdoors it was pushed one stop in development.

Glossary

vein axil	the angle between the vein and midrib of a leaf
bract	a modified leaf beneath a flower head, or at the base of the flower stem
lenticel	a raised pore on a shoot, usually elliptical

left *Lawson Cypress*; right *Leyland Cypress photographed 10 March*

Lawson Cypress at Bedgebury, Kent

Lawson Cypress

Chamaecyparis lawsoniana is a slender, pyramidal, evergreen tree, native to California and Oregon, commonly planted in parks, gardens and cemeteries throughout Britain. Its height can reach 60 metres in the wild although it is generally about half this in cultivation. The male and female flowers open in March and the tiny, round wrinkled cones turn brown when ripe. The minute, scale-like leaves are closely pressed to the twigs and the reddish-brown bark is fissured into deep plates.

Leyland Cypress, × *Cupressocyparis leylandii*, is a hybrid evergreen tree, commonly grown in Britain as a hedge plant or ornamental. Its height has reached 30 metres so far. The male and female flowers are on the same tree, the males shedding pollen in March. The round, scaly, shiny, green-brown cones are small but about twice as large as those on Lawson Cypress.

left *Italian Cypress*; right *Monterey Cypress photographed 10 March*

Italian Cypress in France

Italian Cypress

Cupressus sempervirens is an evergreen tree, native to Mediterranean Europe east to Persia and the Himalayas, which can be found in church-yards and gardens, mainly in southern Britain. Tall and elegant it can live for several hundred years and yields an aromatic, durable wood. Its height reaches 25–45 metres. The male and female flowers open in March and the round shiny-green cones ripen to brown and have 8–14 spiked scales. The blunt-ended, dark-green needles are scale-like and pressed against the twig, and the pinky-brown bark has shallow fissures and ridges.

Monterey Cypress, *Cupressus macrocarpa*, is an evergreen tree, native to Monterey, California, which is commonly found throughout Britain and Europe, planted for ornament and shelter. Its height may reach 38 metres in cultivation but in the wild it is only half that size. It is similar in shape to the Cedar of Lebanon.

Monkey Puzzle at Flimwell, Sussex

Monkey Puzzle photographed 24 July

Monkey Puzzle or Chile Pine

Araucaria araucana is an evergreen tree, native to Chile and Argentina, which was first introduced into Britain in 1795. As it is a very hardy tree and thrives well in deep, moist soil, it is found all over Britain but particularly in the west. It is usually grown, both in Britain and Europe, as an ornamental but interestingly, it is the only conifer from south of the Equator that can grow to timber-producing size in our climate.

Its height reaches 25–30 metres. The male flowers, which open in July, are usually produced on separate trees from the female flowers. These develop into cones which shed their seeds in the August or September of the second year. The leaves are overlapping, densely packed, with horribly prickly scales arranged spirally on the branch. The grey, wrinkled bark has old branch scars or cracks into small, rough plates.

Wellingtonia at Kew

left *Wellingtonia;* right *Coast Redwood photographed 10 March*

Coast Redwood

Sequoia sempervirens is an evergreen conifer, native to the Pacific coast, which is fairly common in large gardens and parks throughout Britain. Its great height, width and longevity (up to 2,000 years) have made this one of the vegetable wonders of the world.

Its height can reach over 90 metres but in Europe it generally reaches about 40 metres. The flowers open in February and the small, brown, oval cones have wrinkled, leathery scales. There are two different kinds of needles: scale-like leaves pressed close to the stem and pointed ones in two rows on each side of the shoots. The soft, orange-red bark is fibrous.

Wellingtonia or **California Big Tree**, *Sequoiadendron giganteum*, is an evergreen conifer, native to California, which is very similar to the Coast Redwood. It can be distinguished from it by its tiny, forward-pointing needles and its cones which take two years to mature.

Yew at Stowting, Kent

Common Yew photographed 16 October

Common Yew or English Yew

Taxus baccata is an evergreen tree, native to Britain, Europe, Iran and Algeria, which can be found in gardens and cemeteries. The hard, durable wood used to be highly valued for timber but now the trees are most commonly grown for ornament, shelter and topiary. Because the yew is the longest lived of all Britain's native trees it has numerous historical and religious associations.

Its height is normally about 25 metres. The male and female flowers, which are almost always produced on separate trees, open in March or April. The fruit, which ripens in mid-September, is a juicy, bright red cup-shaped berry containing a poisonous, nut-like seed. The needles, which vary in length, point well forwards. The purplish-brown bark peels into thin strips with reddish patches.

There is also an upright, cultivated form, 'Fastigiata', the Churchyard Yew, and a golden-leaved form, 'Fastigiata Aureomarginata'.

13

Above *Swamp Cypress;* below *Dawn Redwood photographed 12 August*

Swamp Cypress

Swamp Cypress

Taxodium distichum is a deciduous conifer, native to the south-eastern United States, which is commonly found in parks and gardens in Britain. This hardy, long-lived tree has a lovely feathery foliage that turns dull orange in autumn. Sometimes, cultivated trees growing near water develop 'knees' on the roots, which protrude above water level.

Its height reaches 35–45 metres. The male catkins shed pollen in April and the female conelets develop into round brown cones. The soft, flat needles are evenly arranged in two opposite horizontal rows. The reddish-brown bark is ridged or peeling in fibrous strips and often deeply fluted at the base.

Dawn Redwood, *Metasequoia glyptostroboides*, is a deciduous conifer, similar in leaf shape to Swamp Cypress but distinguishable from it because the branchlets and needles are in alternate pairs and they turn a beautiful red-brown in autumn.

Canadian Hemlock photographed 10 March

Hemlock at Aviemore, Invernessshire

Canadian Hemlock

Tsuga canadensis is an evergreen tree, native to Canada and the north-eastern United States, which was introduced into Britain in 1736. It flourishes in rich, moist soil, and many fine specimens can be found in collections and gardens, particularly in Scotland and the west of Britain. Canadian Hemlock can be distinguished from other members of the species by its large, broad crown and an extra line of needles which grow along the shoot, with their white sides uppermost.

Its height normally reaches about 30 metres and the male and female flowers open in May. The small cones ripen from green to brown in October and the green needles have white undersides and a lemony aroma when crushed. The bark is dark purply-grey and heavily ridged.

Douglas Fir at Canterbury, Kent

Douglas Fir

Douglas Fir

Pseudotsuga menziesii is an evergreen tree, native to western North America from British Columbia to California, which was introduced into Britain in 1827 and is now commonly grown in parks, gardens and plantations all over Britain. In a moist climate and fairly rich soil it grows extremely quickly and produces high quality timber. It can be recognized by its main horizontal branches and its drooping secondary branches.

Its height normally reaches about 60–90 metres. The male and female flowers open in late March and April and the cones, which have straight, pointed bracts, ripen from green to brown. The blunt-tipped needles are dense with a fruity aroma. The bark on strong mature trees is grey- or red-brown, fissured and corky.

Top *Cedar of Lebanon*; centre *Blue Cedar*; bottom *Deodar photographed 10 March*

Cedar of Lebanon at Claremont, Surrey

Cedar of Lebanon

Cedrus libani is an evergreen tree, native to the Near East and Lebanon, which is frequently planted as an ornamental. Its thick trunk and large, horizontal spreading branches make it the most distinctive cedar.

Its height normally reaches 24–36 metres. The male catkins and the female flowers open in November and the wide, barrel-shaped, tapering cones ripen to a purplish-green. The bark is brownish-black and evenly fissured into shallow, flaking ridges.

Deodar, *Cedrus deodar*, has an elegant, pyramidal shape and can be as much as twice the height of the Cedar of Lebanon. **Atlas Cedar**, *Cedrus atlantica*, has less tapering cones and shorter needles than the Cedar of Lebanon. **Blue Cedar**, *Cedrus atlantica* var. *glauca*, is the most commonly cultivated form of the Atlas Cedar. Its foliage ranges from silver-blue to blue-green.

Larches at Invercauld, Aberdeenshire

Common Larch photographed 1 June

Common Larch

Larix decidua is a deciduous conifer, native to the mountains of central and southern Europe, which was first introduced into Britain in the 17th century and is now commonly found in plantations and shelterbelts or as an ornamental in parks and gardens. Tall, fast-growing with horizontal or upward-curving branches, the Common Larch is a beautiful tree which was formerly planted for its timber. However, in recent years it has been largely superceded by the Japanese Larch which grows even more rapidly and in poorer soils.

Its height reaches 30–42 metres. The male and female flowers open in late March or early April. The cones are either long and tapering or short and oval, with wavy scales. The thin, soft needles turn golden-yellow in autumn and the dark pink bark of mature trees is flaky, ridged and fissured.

Noble Firs at Kildrummy, Aberdeenshire

Noble Fir photographed 20 February

Noble Fir

Abies procera is an evergreen tree, native to Washington, Oregon and North California, which was introduced into Britain in 1830 and is now common in Scotland and western England. It flourishes in moist climates and likes deep soil but will also grow in cold, exposed positions. It is planted both as an ornamental and for its close-grained timber which is used in building.

Its height normally reaches 45–60 metres but is sometimes rather less in cultivation. The male and female flowers open in May and the long cones are almost covered with yellow, downward pointing bracts. Even relatively small trees can produce a profusion of large, erect cones. The pale grey or purplish bark is smooth with a few deep, dark cracks.

Santa Lucia Fir

Abies bracteata is an evergreen tree, native to the Santa Lucia Mountains in California, but grown infrequently as an ornamental tree in Britain.

Its height normally reaches 45 metres although it usually only achieves about 25 metres in British specimens. The male and female flowers open in May and the cones have spines protruding from its bracts. The needles have sharp points and the smooth black or purplish bark has blisters and cracks around the knots.

Greek Fir, *Abies cephalonica*, is an evergreen tree, native to the mountains of southern Greece and planted for ornament in large gardens in Britain. It is easily recognised because the needles radiate from all round the shoot and the buds are resinous. Its height reaches about 45–49 metres. The male and female flowers open in April. The greeny-brown cones have bracts and the dark brown to grey bark breaks into small plates.

Red Fir, *Abies magnifica*, is a large, beautifully symmetrical, evergreen tree, native to Oregon and California, which is sometimes grown as an ornamental in large gardens in Britain and Europe. Its height can reach 65 metres but British specimens usually only reach 30–35 metres. The male and female flowers are produced in May and the large, barrel-shaped cones are sparse. The needles are curved and the purple or grey, corky bark has curled cracks and dark branch scars as it ages.

Forrest's Silver Fir, *Abies delavayi* var. *forrestii*, is an evergreen tree, native to southern China, which is found in large collections in Britain. Its height reaches 49 metres in the wild but cultivated specimens usually only reach 20 metres. The male and female flowers open in late April, the buds are resinous and the deep-blue, barrel-shaped cones have bracts. The long, shiny green needles are deeply knotched with white bands underneath.

Korean Fir, *Abies koreana*, is a small, bushy, evergreen tree, native to Korea, which is often grown in British gardens because it produces lovely purply-blue cones at a young age. Its height normally reaches about 9 metres and the male and female flowers open in May. The ripe, cylindrical cones exude blobs of white resin and the blunt, notched needles are shorter than those on other silver firs. The shiny, brown-black bark is covered with lenticels.

Caucasian Fir, *Abies nordmanniana*, is. an evergreen fir, native to the Caucasus, and grown for ornament in collections and gardens in Britain. Its height can reach 50–60 metres. The male and female flowers open in late April and the resinous cones have downward turning bracts. The slightly aromatic needles form two rows giving a dense appearance to the foliage. The smooth, grey bark develops square plates and fissures in age.

Opposite page. Top to bottom *Santa Lucia Fir; Greek Fir; Red Fir; Forrest's Silver Fir; Korean Fir; Caucasian Fir photographed 20 February*

Norway Spruce photographed 1 June

Norway Spruce in Finland

Norway Spruce

Picea abies in an evergreen tree, native to northern Scandinavia, north-west Russia and central Europe, which is also grown throughout northern Europe and the eastern United States. It was probably introduced into Britain in the 16th century and it is common in parks, gardens and plantations. The timber (white deal) is used for roofing and paper pulp but the young trees are most widely known in Britain because of their cultivation as Christmas trees.

Its height normally reaches about 36 metres or taller and its male and female flowers open in May. The cones are quite large and slender, developing from green to glossy brown in the autumn, and the hard, dark green needles point strongly forward. The red-brown bark of younger trees flakes into scales but on older trees it turns dark purple and breaks into shallow plates.

Sitka Spruce at Canterbury, Kent

Sitka Spruce photographed 1 June

Sitka Spruce

Picea sitchensis is an evergreen tree, native to the entire west coast of North America, which was introduced into Britain in 1831 and now grows abundantly in the north and west. As it flourishes particularly well in continuously damp soils and a cool, humid climate, producing timber more quickly, yet of equal quality to the Norway Spruce, it is extensively planted commercially. It can be easily distinguished from the Norway Spruce because its cones have wavy-edged scales and are shorter and stubbier.

Its height normally reaches about 50 metres in Britain although it grows to 75 metres in its native range. The male and female flowers open in May. The pale green cones turn almost white by autumn and feel soft when squeezed but the four-sided needles are prickly. The bark cracks with age, turning purplish-grey and breaking into plates.

Morinda Spruce or West Himalayan Spruce

Picea smithiana is an evergreen tree, native to the western Himalayas, which is common in collections and large gardens in Britain. It is easily recognised by its long, outward-pointing needles and drooping branchlets.

Its height normally reaches about 36 metres but it can grow to 70 metres. The male and female flowers open in early May and the longish cones become notched in maturity. The purple-grey bark cracks into shallow plates.

Brewer's Weeping Spruce, *Picea breweriana*, is an evergreen tree, native to California and Oregon, which is uncommon in Britain but its long, curtained branchlets make it a most graceful ornamental for gardens. Its height normally reaches about 15 metres but it can grow to 36 metres in the wild. The male and female flowers open in May and the purple to brown cones have rounded scales. The needles all round the shoot point forwards, and the dark, pink-grey bark peels into round, curling plates.

Colorado Spruce, *Picea pungens*, is an evergreen tree, native to the Rocky Mountains of the United States, but rare in Britain. Its height normally reaches 30–45 metres. The male and female flowers open in May. The pale brown cones have wavy, toothed scales and the four-sided needles are spine-tipped when young, becoming blunter with age. The purplish-grey bark splits into coarse scales.

Oriental Spruce or **Caucasian Spruce**, *Picea orientalis*, is an evergreen tree, native to the Caucasus and Asia Minor, and often grown in British gardens for ornament. Its height normally reaches 30 metres and the male and female flowers open in late April. The young purple cones ripen to brown. The needles are much shorter than on other spruces. The pinkish-brown bark breaks into small, curling plates.

Honda Spruce, *Picea jezoensis* var. *hondoenis*, is an evergreen tree, native to Japan but grown commonly in collections and gardens in Britain. Its height normally reaches about 15 metres although it grows to 28 metres in the wild. The male and female flowers open in May and the cones have notched, inward-curving scales. The pine-tipped needles thrust upwards and forwards and the brown or grey bark cracks into plates.

Likiang Spruce, *Picea likiangensis*, is an evergreen tree, native to western China and Tibet but grown in Britain as an ornamental. Its height reaches 45 metres in the wild but hardly more than 20 metres in Britain. The male and female flowers open in April and the cones have round, wavy scales. The four-sided needles vary in colour with the upper ones thrusting forward. The pale grey bark is rough with long, dark fissures.

Opposite page. Top left to bottom right *Morinda Spruce; Brewer's Weeping Spruce; Colorado Spruce; Oriental Spruce; Honda Spruce; Likiang Spruce photographed 20 February*

Scots Pine at Whitehaugh, Aberdeenshire

Scots Pine photographed 16 October

Scots Pine

Pinus sylvestris is an evergreen tree, native to Scotland and growing abundantly where re-introduced in the south and east of England. Because it flourishes in a wide variety of soils and climates it is planted extensively in Europe and North America for timber and ornament.

Its height normally reaches 30–36 metres. The round, yellow male flowers and the red female flowers open in May and the cones ripen late in the second year, turning from green to red-brown. The stiff, twisted, blue-green needles are born in pairs. The bark is finely cracked into large plates, brown on young trees and turning flaky orange on the upper trunk and branches of mature trees.

Corsican Pine at Kew

Austrian Pine photographed 10 March

Austrian Pine

Pinus nigra var. *nigra* is an evergreen tree, native to middle and eastern Europe. Because of its broad crown, wide-spreading branches and readiness to grow in poor or chalky soils, it has become commonly planted in Britain for ornament or as a shelter tree.

Its height reaches 30–33 metres. The golden-yellow male flowers and the pinky-red female flowers open in late May. The cones develop to a glossy brown during the second year, and the scales open to release winged seeds. The stiff, dark green needles are borne in pairs and the browny-black bark splits into scaly plates.

Corsican Pine, *Pinus nigra* var. *maritima*, is an evergreen tree, native to Corsica, Sicily and southern Italy, which is commonly planted in Britain for timber and for shelter. It is distinguished from the other varieties of *Pinus nigra* by its pinky-orange, fissured bark.

Stone Pine photographed 16 October

Stone Pine in France

Stone Pine

Pinus pinea is an evergreen tree, native to southern Europe, but cultivated in Britain for the last four centuries. Highly valued on the Continent for its kidney-shaped seeds which are eaten either raw, or cooked, the tree is distinguished by its thick, spreading, umbrella-shaped crown, which is often broader than its height. Although a characteristic feature of the Mediterranean landscape, it is short-lived as the young plants tend to be killed by severe frost.

Its height varies from 13–30 metres, depending on where it grows. The golden male flowers and the yellowish-green female flowers open in June, but the smooth, glossy, pale brown, egg-shaped cones, which grow to about 12cm long, remain closed for three years. The pairs of thick, dark green needles are twisted, pointed and rather sparse. The reddish-brown bark forms long plates with deep, dark cracks.

Aleppo Pine in France

Aleppo Pine photographed 16 October

Aleppo Pine

Pinus halepensis is an evergreen tree, native to southern Europe from Spain to Asia Minor, which occurs only rarely in Britain in the south. With its dome-shaped crown and contorted branches it is common on drier mountain soils and by the sea and there are specimens as high as 26 metres on the Dalmatian Coast. Although its wood has little value, the resin yields oil of turpentine and is also used in making Retsina, the Greek wine.

Its height normally reaches about 15 metres. The red-brown female flowers open in May and the orange to purple-brown cones, which are borne in pairs or threes, remain on the branches for several years. The growth buds are free of resin and recurved. The long slender needles are borne in pairs and fall in the second or third years. The dark, purple-brown bark has broad orange cracks.

Arolla Pine at Kew

Arolla Pine photographed 16 October

Arolla Pine

Pinus cembra is an evergreen tree native to southern and central Europe from France and Switzerland to Poland and Rumania, which grows on dry slopes in the Alps, the Tatras and the Carpathians, usually not above 1,500 metres. It was introduced into Britain before 1746 but is still rare except in collections.

In the wild it normally reaches about 25 metres in height and the largest specimens in cultivation are around 30 metres high. The yellow male flowers open in early summer and the ripe cones are egg-shaped, 5–8cm long, and don't open on the tree but fall with the seeds still inside. The needles are 5–8cm long and persist for 3–5 years. The bark is dark reddish-grey and very rough.

Five Needled Pines

David's Pine, *Pinus armandii*, is an evergreen tree, native to China, Korea and Formosa, which was introduced into Britain in 1897. There are a few trees in Scotland but it is uncommon in England and Ireland.

Its height reaches about 22.5 metres. The male and female flowers open in June and the cones, which are at first green, develop to an orange-brown colour. The broad, barrel-shaped, thick-scaled cone distinguishes it from the other five-needled pines. The long needles, in bunches of five, are often bent or crinkled at the base, shiny green on the outside and paler green on the inside. The twigs are bare in places and covered with drops of resin. The smooth bark is dull pink to purple-grey, cracking deeply into flaky, square plates.

Mexican White Pine, *Pinus ayacahuite*, is an evergreen tree, native to Mexico and Guatemala, which was introduced to Britain in 1840 but is uncommon except in collections. It grows in sheltered valleys and on moist mountain slopes at altitudes of 2,500 to 3,000 metres. Its height normally reaches about 30 metres. The male and female flowers open in June and the long pointed cones turn pale brown and open as they ripen. The slender needles are in clusters of five and the mature bark is reddish-brown with shallow fissures.

Macedonian Pine, *Pinus peuce*, is an evergreen tree, native to the Balkans, which was introduced into Britain in 1864 and is now found in many collections and large gardens. Slender and densely branched, it is an extremely sturdy tree which grows slowly but steadily in most soils. Its height normally reaches about 36 metres and the male and female flowers open in early June. The long, green cones ripen to red-brown in September, exuding drops of resin and the scales open wide in early autumn to release the winged seeds. The needles, in clusters of five, point strongly forwards and the bark on the mature trees is either dark purple or grey and fissured.

Himalayan Pine, *Pinus wallichiana*, is an evergreen tree, native to the Himalayas, which was introduced into Britain in 1823 and is now commonly found in parks, gardens and churchyards. It is a hardy tree which grows well in sandy loam, sheltered from wind. Its height normally reaches 35–45 metres and its male and female flowers open in May. The long banana-shaped cones develop in the second year and are covered in resin. The short, thick needles are borne in pairs and the bark is orange-brown and sometimes cracked into plates.

Opposite page. Top left to bottom right *Himalayan Pine; Mexican White Pine; Macedonian Pine; David's Pine photographed 20 February*

Above *pollarded willows in winter in Somerset;* below *White Willow in France*

left *Crack Willow;* right *White Willow photographed 24 July*

White Willow

Salix alba is a deciduous tree, native to Britain, Europe, northern Asia and northern Africa, which grows along riversides and in valleys. Its height reaches 25 metres. The yellow male and green female catkins open in May and the fruiting catkins release white, fluffy seeds in June. The dark green leaves are covered in white, silky hairs with thick white felt on the undersides. The dark grey bark has a network of ridges.

Crack Willow, *Salix fragilis*, is a deciduous tree, native to Britain, Europe, Russia and south-west Asia, which grows on river banks. It is allied to the White Willow and often hybridises with it but its branches are more wide-spreading, the leaves are larger and hairless, and the catkins are longer.

Weeping Willow, *Saix* × *chrysocoma*, is a deciduous hybrid, famed for its drooping, slender shoots and golden foliage.

Eucalyptus at Kew

Eucalyptus gunnii *photographed 12 August*

Eucalyptus

Eucalyptus gunnii is an evergreen tree, native to Tasmania, which was introduced into Britain in the mid-19th century and is now found planted for ornament in many parks and gardens.

Its height normally reaches about 30 metres in the wild, although those in cultivation can grow taller and those in unfavourable conditions may be much smaller and stunted. The flowers, normally in threes, open in July and August, and the tiny, urn-shaped fruits enclose a seed. The peculiarity of Eucalyptus is that the leaves produced during the juvenile phase are markedly different from those produced during the adult phase and this young foliage can be prolonged by regular pruning. The juvenile leaves are stalkless, rounded and clasp the stem in pairs; the alternate adult leaves are long and thin, on a slender stalk. The smooth pink bark peels in large flakes exposing cream-coloured wood which darkens to grey-brown as it ages.

Southern Nettle-tree in France

Southern Nettle-tree photographed 24 July

Southern Nettle-tree

Celtis australis is a deciduous tree, native to southern Europe and south-west Asia, which was introduced into Britain in the 16th century but has only occasionally been planted in parks for shade or ornament. It tends to be affected by frost which stunts its growth over the years making survival difficult. Its timber is used in carpentry and joinery and for charcoal, and the bark yields a yellow dye.

Its height reaches 15–21 metres. The male and female flowers occur on the same tree and open in May. The small globular fruits on slender stalks ripen to a reddish-brown in autumn and are edible. The roughly-textured, coarsely-toothed leaves are shiny on the upper surface and downy underneath. The smooth grey bark is similar to beech bark.

Above *Medlar;* below *Quince photographed 23 May*

Medlar photographed 20 October   *Quince photographed 24 October*

Medlar, Quince

Cydonia oblonga is a deciduous tree, probably native to central Asia and the Near East, which was introduced into Britain centuries ago. Its wonderfully fragrant fruit is hard and acid when raw but delicious cooked in jams or jellies. Its height reaches 4–6 metres. The pink or white flowers open in May and the yellow, pear-shaped fruit is usually covered with white felt. The leaves are dark green above and covered with grey felt underneath.

Medlar, *Mespilus germanica*, is a deciduous tree, native to south-east Europe and Asia Minor, which has been cultivated for centuries in British orchards for its fruit. Its height reaches 6 metres. The white or pinkish flowers open in late May and the apple-shaped fruits have a large 'open' end. The leaves are downy and older trees may bear thorns.

Wild Cherry at Polstead, Suffolk

Wild Cherry photographed 14 July

Wild Cherry or Gean

Prunus avium is a deciduous tree, native to Britain and Europe, which can be found growing in hedges, woods, gardens and parks, and it has also been cultivated and naturalised in eastern North America. Although the fruit tends to be bitter this is one of the parents of cultivated fruiting cherries, particularly the black varieties.

Its height normally reaches about 18 metres. The clusters of white blossoms open in mid-April and the round, light or blackish-red fruits are sweet or bitter but not acid. The strongly-veined, coarsely-toothed leaves are hairy along the veins on the under surface and the yellow stalks are reddish on top and yellow below, with glands near the leaf base. They colour yellow and red in autumn. The shiny, red-brown bark has clearly marked lenticels in horizontal lines, broken by large cracks.

Bird Cherry photographed 1 June

Bird Cherry on Deeside, Aberdeenshire

Bird Cherry

Prunus padus is a deciduous tree or shrub, native to Britain, Europe and Asia, which is often planted in streets and gardens. It is a very hardy tree that grows in most soils and has given rise to a number of varieties. Its timber is valued by cabinet-makers. Although 'Plena' and 'Watereri' are the two most popular cultivars planted in gardens, this tree too has a very pretty aspect.

Its height reaches to 15 metres. The fragrant, white flowers open in late May, on spikes. The shiny, black fruits are small, round and bitter and ripen in July and August. The finely-toothed leaves are rounded at the base, dull green on the surface with tufts of down underneath in the vein axils. The smooth, dark, greyish-brown bark has a strong, rather acrid smell.

White Cherry 'Tai Haku' at Windsor

Flowering Cherries

Prunus serrulata comprises a group of deciduous, ornamental, flowering cherries which have been developed in Japan since the 17th century. Their origin is obscure but most are thought to derive from the Oshima Cherry, *Prunus speciosa*.

Kanzan is the most widely planted flowering cherry. It has purply-rose double flowers and bronze foliage. **Mikurama-gaeshi** has gaunt, ascending branches and large, single or semi-double, delicate pink flowers. **Shirotae** is a dense, spreading tree with fragrant, white, semi-double flowers and leaves with teeth that have long hair-like tips, creating a fringed appearance. **Tai-Haku** has wide-spreading branches and pure white flowers. The leaves are red-bronze when young, yellow or orange in autumn. **Ukon** is an upright, sparsely-branched tree with semi-double, pale greenish flowers. *Prunus × yedoensis* has wide-spreading, downward curving branches and produces numerous, slightly perfumed, white or pink flowers.

Opposite page. Top left to bottom right *'Kanzan'; 'Ukon'; 'Mikuramagaeshi'; 'Shirotae'; 'Tai Haku'; × yedoensis photographed 24 April*

Top *Crab Apple*; centre *Japanese Crab*; below *Purple Crab photographed 13 May*

Above *Purple crab;* below *Wild Crab photographed 13 October*

Crab Apple or Wild Crab

Malus sylvestris is a deciduous tree, native to Britain, Europe and south-west Asia, which is found in hedgerows, copses and thickets and it is one of the parents of the Orchard Apples.

Its height reaches 9 metres. The white or pale pinky-white flowers open in late May and the small, round, hard, sour fruits ripen to a yellowy-green, flushed with orangey-red in September. The finely-toothed leaves have a reddish stalk and some branches are thorny. The brown bark is fissured.

Siberian Crab, *Malus baccata*, is a deciduous tree, native to Siberia and North China, which has white flowers. **Japanese Crab**, *Malus floribunda*, is probably a hybrid, native to Japan, which has rose-red and pale pink flowers. **Purple Crab**, *Malus × purpurea*, is a commonly planted hybrid with reddish-purple flowers, leaves and apples.

Common Pear photographed 13 October

Young flowering Pear at Windsor

Common Pear

Pyrus communis is a deciduous tree, probably of hybrid origin, which is found growing wild in many parts of Britain and Europe. This complex species includes the Wild Pear which was hybridised to form the Orchard Pears. These then escaped back to the wild and interbred with the ancestral Wild Pear so that it is now virtually impossible to distinguish them from one another. Although the Wild Pear is graceful, with hanging branches and a profusion of flowers, the cultivated varieties are just as pretty with the added advantage of bearing edible fruits too.

Its height reaches about 12 metres. The white flower clusters open in late April or early May and the round fruits ripen to a yellow-green with sweet-tasting flesh. The shiny green leaves are variable, being either hairless to start with, or becoming so later, and the dark brown bark is broken into small, thick, plates.

Above *Service Tree of Fontainbleau;* below *Wild Service Tree photographed 26 August*

Service Tree of Fontainbleau at Kew

Wild Service Tree

Sorbus torminalis is a deciduous tree, native to Britain, Europe, North Africa and south-west Asia. The distinctive feature of this tree is its leaves which are similar to a maple's. Its height normally reaches 10–13 metres. The white flowers, on very downy stalks, open in late May or June and the brownish, speckled fruits ripen in September. The shiny, dark green leaves are double-toothed with 3 or 5 lobes and colour deep red in autumn. The dark brown or grey bark cracks into scaly plates.

Service Tree of Fontainbleau, *Sorbus latifolia*, is a deciduous tree, native to western and central Europe, which is thought to derive from a hybrid between *Sorbus torminalis* and a whitebeam. Its height reaches 18 metres. The white flowers open in May and the shiny, oval leaves have grey felt underneath and a downy stalk. The dark brown bark is shaggy and peeling.

Above *Whitebeam;* below *Swedish Whitebeam photographed 26 August*

Whitebeam near Wye, Kent, in a gale

Whitebeam
Sorbus aria is a deciduous tree, native to Britain and central and southern
Europe, which is planted in parks and streets. Its height reaches to 25
metres. The yellowish-white flowers open in May and the small round
fruits ripen to scarlet in September. Roughly-toothed leaves are covered
with thick white felt on the underside and turn yellow and brown in the
autumn. The smooth grey bark develops shallow ridges.

Swedish Whitebeam, *Sorbus intermedia*, is a deciduous tree, native to
Scandinavia, USSR and north-east Germany, which is often planted on
council estates because it can withstand pollution. Its height reaches to 10
metres. The dull white flowers open in May and the fruits ripen to
orange-red or reddish-brown in September. The toothed, lobed leaves
have thick white felt on the underside and the smooth, purply-grey bark is
fissured.

Magnolia campbelli at Windsor

Magnolia

Magnolia × soulangiana is a deciduous hybrid tree and the most popular magnolia grown in Britain. Its height can eventually reach 7.5 metres. The large-petalled flowers, which are white on the inside and pinky-mauve on the outside, open in late April and continue to develop until June. The glossy, tapering leaves are downy on the underside. There is a pure white form 'Alba' and also a much more strongly red form 'Rustica Rubra'.

Northern Japanese Magnolia, *Magnolia kobus*, is a deciduous tree, larger than *M. × soulangiana* (its height reaches 12 metres) but with smaller leaves. **Evergreen Magnolia**, *Magnolia grandiflora*, is a large evergreen tree which reaches to 30 metres and flowers from July onwards.

Opposite page. Above Magnolia kobus; centre M. × soulangiana *'Rustica rubra'*; below Magnolia × soulangiana *photographed 24 April*

Above left *Antartic Beech;* right *Roble Beech;* below *Dombey's Southern Beech*

Roble Beech at Kew

Roble Beech

Nothofagus obliqua is a deciduous tree, native to Chile and western Argentina, which together with Raoul, *Northofagus procera*, has been planted in Britain to replace dead elms. Its height reaches 30 metres. The flowers open in May and the fruits release their nutlets in September. The toothed leaves have 7–11 pairs of veins and the smooth, grey bark has dark fissures and cracks later into square, curved flakes.

Dombey's Southern Beech, *Nothofagus dombeyi*, is an evergreen tree, native to Chile, which is sometimes grown in large parks in Britain. It is distinguished by its glossy, evergreen, wrinkled leaves with 4 pairs of veins.

Antarctic Beech, *Nothofagus antarctica*, is a deciduous tree, native to southern Chile, which is occasionally grown in gardens in Britain. It is distinguished by its small leaves which have only 4 pairs of veins.

Wych Elm photographed 1 June

Wych Elm at Castle Forbes, Aberdeenshire

Wych Elm

Ulmus glabra is a deciduous tree, native to Europe and west Asia and Britain, where it is commonly found in the north and west. Its strong trunk and domed crown make it an excellent tree for cultivation in parks and estates, both for shelter and for ornament, and it can thrive even in polluted areas where the soil is poor.

Its height can reach 41 metres. The dense, stalkless flower clusters open in early March and the fruits, which each contain a single seed, ripen to pale brown and fall in July. The double-toothed leaves are always lop-sided at the base, with very short stalks. The upper surface is rough, the underneath softly hairy, and each leaf has 14–20 pairs of veins. The smooth grey bark of younger trees cracks, furrows and turns brownish on mature trees.

Elm flowers photographed 14 March

English Elm at Sellindge, Kent

English Elm

Ulmus procera is a deciduous tree, native to Britain, which could once be found commonly in fields, parks, streets and hedgerows but over the last 50 years it has been decimated by Dutch Elm disease so that very few healthy elms can now be found. Tall and broad, with a rich billowing foliage on distinct groups of branches, it has long been one of our most beautiful native trees. As the seeds are rarely fertile, it propagates mainly via sucker shoots.

Its height reaches about 30 metres. The reddish flower clusters open in early March and the small fruits, containing the seed near the tip, are set by April or May. The rough, dark green, veined leaves have a short, downy stalk and white down along the main vein underneath. The dark brown bark is ridged and furrowed.

Caucasian Elm at Kew

Caucasian Elm photographed 17 May

Caucasian Elm

Zelkova carpinifolia is a deciduous tree, native to Iran and the Caucasus mountains, which was probably introduced into Britain in 1760 and is now planted as an ornamental in large gardens and parks. It has a short trunk which divides into many erect, crowded and dense branches that spread outwards at their tips. The timber is hard and durable and although it is slow growing at first it is a hardy and long-lived tree with a very distinctive and interesting aspect.

Its height reaches to about 35 metres. The male and female flowers open in April and the pea-sized fruits are lumpy with 4 ridges on top. The dark green, coarsely-toothed leaves have 6–12 pairs of veins and are sometimes hairy on the upper surface and downy on the undersides. The smooth, grey bark splits into scales exposing orange or pinky bark beneath.

left *Cut-leaved Beech;* centre *Beech;* right *Purple Beech photographed 27 September*

Beech

Common Beech

Fagus sylvatica is a deciduous tree, native to southern Britain and Europe, which is commonly cultivated for ornament, shade and timber. Its form varies from tall and columnar if grown in woodland, to wide and spreading if planted in an isolated position.

Its height reaches to 30 metres. The male and female flowers open in May and the fruits ripen in autumn to release triangular, husked nuts. The young leaves are a shimmering green with 5–9 pairs of veins, turning to lovely shades of orange and brown in October. The smooth bark is grey.

Weeping Beech, *Fagus sylvatica* forma *pendula*, has masses of drooping, pendulous branches. **Purple Beech**, *Fagus sylvatica* forma *purpurea*, has beautiful purple leaves and the nuts have a pinky-brown tint.

Above left *Eastern Hop Hornbeam*; below right *Common Hornbeam photographed
27 September*

Common Hornbeam at Sellindge, Kent

Common Hornbeam

Carpinus betulus is a deciduous tree, native to south-east Britain, Europe and Asia Minor, which is cultivated for timber or as a hedge, park or street tree. Sometimes mistaken for beech it is, in fact, more graceful with a vertically fluted trunk. Its height reaches 20–30 metres. The fruiting catkins open in March and are produced in facing pairs with the nuts at the base of the bract. The dark green, toothed and veined leaves turn yellow in autumn. The bark is brown.

Eastern Hop Hornbeam, *Ostrya virginiana*, is a deciduous tree, native to eastern North America, which is sometimes cultivated for ornament in Britain. Its height reaches 9–18 metres. The catkins open in April and the fruits develop on long, hairy stalks. The leaves are hairy on the upper surface, downy beneath.

European Hop Hornbeam, *Ostrya carpinifolia*, has smaller fruits and more ribbed leaves than the Eastern Hop Hornbeam.

left *Downy Birch;* right *Silver Birch photographed 26 August*

Birches at Whitehaugh, Aberdeenshire

Silver Birch

Betula pendula is a deciduous tree, native to Britain, Europe and Asia Minor, which is planted in gardens for its beautiful, pendulous form, or in plantations to protect other young trees. Its height normally reaches 18 metres although occasionally it can reach 30 metres. The male and female catkins open in early April at the same time as the leaves. The leaves are double-toothed and wedge-shaped at the base without down. The white bark has thin, horizontal lines and large, diamond-shaped cracks in older trees.

Downy Birch, *Betula pubescens*, is also a native deciduous tree, originally classed with Silver Birch and similar to it in many ways. The main differences are that the branches are not pendulous, the shoots, twigs and leaves are downy, the leaves are single-toothed and the bark has no diamond-shaped cracks.

Sweet Chestnut photographed 27 September

Sweet Chestnut at Wivenhoe, Essex

Sweet Chestnut

Castanea sativa is a deciduous tree, native to southern Europe, North Africa and Asia Minor, which was introduced to Britain by the Romans and is now found growing naturally in the south or cultivated for ornament in parks and gardens in the Midlands and further north. Relished by Europeans for their delicious nuts, our weather is not generally hot enough to encourage a good chestnut harvest. In every other respect the tree has adapted admirably to our climate.

Its height reaches 30 metres and its girth is sometimes 10 metres or more. Its male and female flowers, which open in late June or July, generally occur on the same stalk and are pollinated by insects rather than the wind. One to four red-brown nuts are encased in a prickly burr and ripen in September. The dark brown bark is ridged, often spirally.

Above *Italian Alder*; below *Common Alder photographed 10 March*

Common Alder on Loch Lomond

Common Alder

Alnus glutinosa is a deciduous tree, native to Britain, Europe, West Asia and North Africa, which grows wild in damp places. Its height can reach 20–25 metres. Its male catkins shed pollen in early March and the small, green, egg-shaped fruits turn woody in winter. The rounded leaves have an indented tip and 6–8 pairs of veins, each with long tufts of down in the vein axils underneath. The dark brown bark splits into plates.

Italian Alder, *Alnus cordata*, is a deciduous tree, native to southern Italy and Corsica, which is planted for ornament in Britain. Its height reaches 15 metres. The long male catkins shed pollen between February and April. The green, egg-shaped fruit, which usually occurs in threes, is much longer than on other alders. The finely-toothed, glossy green leaves have 5 or 6 pairs of veins with tufts of down in the vein axils underneath. The smooth, grey bark is covered with lenticels and cracks.

Black Poplar photographed 18 May

Black Poplar in France   *Lombardy Poplar in France*

Black Poplar

Populus nigra is a deciduous tree, native to north and western Europe, which is not now frequently found in its true form although the numerous hybrids which have sprung from it are often planted around railways, factories, roads, parks and gardens. Its height reaches 30 metres or more. The male catkins shed pollen in March and the female catkins shed woolly, white seeds in June. The oval to diamond-shaped leaves are shiny green turning yellow in autumn and the grey-brown bark is fissured and ridged.

Lombardy Poplar, *Populus nigra* cv. 'Italica', is a deciduous tree, native to Lombardy in northern Italy. The most distinctive characteristic of this tree is its tall, slender, plume-like shape. The individual twigs follow the upward thrust of the trunk so there are no large branches or true crown; this unusual characteristic is known as 'fastigiate' and is found occasionally in many kinds of trees.

Grey Poplar at Westonbirt Arboretum, Gloucestershire

left *White Poplar;* right *Grey Poplar photographed 14 July*

White Poplar

Populus alba is a deciduous tree which has been planted in Britain as an ornamental and for shelter near the sea, as it withstands salt spray. Its most distinctive feature is its white bark and the white down which covers the winter twigs, buds and young leaves. Its height can reach 30 metres but it usually only grows to 20 metres in Britain. The male and female flowers open in April and the fruiting catkins release cottony seeds in June. The lobed leaves become dark glossy green on the upper surface and remain white underneath. The smooth, white bark has diamond-shaped marks but is black and rough at the base.

Grey Poplar, *Populus canescens*, is a deciduous tree, thought to be a natural hybrid between the White Poplar and the Aspen. Its leaves are circular, like the Aspen, and their undersurfaces are covered in grey rather than white down. The catkins are longer than those of the White Poplar but the bark is similar.

Aspen in Finland

Aspen photographed 14 July

Aspen

Populus tremula is a deciduous tree, native to Britain, Europe, North Africa and Asia, which, in the wild, is most frequently seen in thickets because it suckers easily. It is a very hardy tree which flourishes best in moist, clay soil. Its most famous and distinguishing characteristic is the perpetual quiver of its leaves, caused by the slender, flattened leafstalks which tremble in the slightest breeze.

Its height normally reaches 15 metres. The long, hairy, caterpillar-like male and female catkins open in February and the fruiting catkins ripen in May. The grey-green leaves are either broadly oval with wavy edges or wedge-shaped. On vigorous shoots the leaves have a pair of glands where they join the stem; these turn yellow in autumn. The smooth, grey bark has horizontal lines.

Judas Tree in southern France

Judas Tree showing flowers emerging from the trunk photographed 18 May

Judas Tree

Cercis siliquastrum is a deciduous tree, native to southern Europe and the eastern Mediterranean, which was introduced into Britain in the 16th century and is planted for ornament, mainly in the south as it loves the sun. Its rosy-purple flowers blossom in profusion during May, making this one of the most lovely flowering trees for the garden. Its popular name is derived from the legend that this was the tree from which Judas hung himself.

Its height can reach to 12 metres but it is usually lower with more than one stem, rather than a distinct trunk. The purple-rose flower clusters are produced in the old branches' joints and each flower has a slender stalk. The pea-shaped fruit pods are flat, developing from green to rosy-purple and remain on the tree during winter. The smooth, roundish leaves are arranged alternately along the shoots.

Common Lime photographed 14 July

Lime at Alford, Aberdeenshire

Common Lime

Tilea × europaea is a deciduous tree, thought to be a natural hybrid between two wild limes: *Tilia cordata* and *Tilia platyphyllos*. Its origin is not properly known but it is the most common lime found in Britain and is widely planted in streets and gardens for shade and ornament. Despite its pretty foliage and fragrant flowers it is prone to attack by aphids, which deposit a sticky resin on the leaves. This turns black in late summer and can drop on to unsuspecting passers-by. Another distinctive feature is the numerous suckers which develop at the base and form burrs on the trunk.

Its height reaches about 39 metres. The fragrant clusters of yellowy-white flowers open in early July and pollination occurs by insects (lime honey is prized by beekeepers). The pale green, heart-shaped leaves are smooth with toothed edges and long stalks. The pale grey bark is smooth and fibrous.

Black Mulberry photographed 2 August

White Mulberry in southern France, pollarded for silk farming

White Mulberry

Morus alba is a deciduous tree, native to China but cultivated for centuries in other eastern countries and southern Europe for silkworm manufacture. Its height reaches about 9 metres. The male and female flowers, in separate catkins, are produced in May. The fruits are generally white or pink, but occasionally purple, and the shiny leaves are less downy than the Common Mulberry.

Common or **Black Mulberry**, *Morus nigra*, is a deciduous tree, probably native to the Far East, but naturalised for so many centuries in Europe that its origins are unknown. Its height usually reaches 9 metres. The male and female flowers are in separate catkins and the long fruits ripen to dark red. The heart-shaped leaves are rough and hairy on the surface and downy underneath.

Indian Bean Tree photographed 14 July

Indian Bean or Southern Catalpa

Catalpa bignonioides is a deciduous tree, native to the eastern United States, which was first introduced into Britain in 1726 and is now cultivated in parks and gardens, particularly in the south, and throughout Europe. It is a hardy tree that flourishes best in deep, moist soil and an open, sunny situation. It has a rounded, many-branched crown and wide-spreading branches down the trunk.

Its height normally reaches between 8–15 metres. The white-frilled flowers open in June and July, and the long, slender, pencil-like fruit pods turn brown in autumn and release their white, papery seeds the following spring. The large leaves are shiny green on the upper surface with pale down underneath. These unfurl at the end of June, turning black by the autumn. The pinky-brown or grey bark is flaky or ridged.

Foxglove Tree in southern France

Foxglove Tree photographed 18 May

Foxglove-tree

Paulownia tomentosa is a deciduous tree, native to China, which was introduced into Britain in 1838 and is now cultivated in parks and gardens although it is more successfully planted in Japan and Europe. It has a rounded crown and thick, stiff, open branches, with almost all parts rather downy. Because it produces its flowerbuds during the autumn and they are exposed throughout the winter they frequently fail to flower in colder climates. However, in warmer areas the beautiful, foxglove-shaped blossoms make this an outstanding flowering tree.

Its height reaches to 12 metres. The upright flower clusters open in May and the numerous winged seeds are contained in an oval capsule that dries and then splits to release the fruit. The leaves are very variable, some oval, some lobed, with silky hairs on the upper surface and soft, grey down underneath.

Common Holly; below leaves of Highclere Holly cultivars photographed 26 October

Common Holly at Churchingford, Somerset

Common Holly

Ilex aquifolium is a broadleaved, evergreen tree, native to Britain, Europe and west Asia, which is commonly planted in hedges, for ornament and shelter, throughout the British Isles. Its bright red berries and prickly leaves are a traditional European Christmas decoration. Its height reaches 25 metres. The minute white flowers open in May and ripen to tiny four-seeded red berries in November. The tough, waxy, glossy, wavy leaves have sharp spines but these decrease on higher branches and in mature trees. The smooth grey bark has some dark marks.

Highclere Holly, *Ilex × altaclarensis*, is a group of evergreen hybrids between *Ilex aquifolium* and *Ilex perado*, from which many cultivars have been produced – most with larger, less prickly leaves and bigger flowers and berries.

Common Hawthorn in southern France

Hawthorns; above left *'Paul's Scarlet';* above right *Midland Hawthorn;* below left *'Plena' photographed 28 May*

Common Hawthorn

Crataegus monogyna is a deciduous tree, native to Britain and Europe as far as Afghanistan, which is commonly used for making hedges because of its dense, thorny growth. Its height reaches about 10 metres. The fragrant flowers open in mid-May and the red, single-stoned fruits ripen in September. The 5- or 7-lobed leaves are shiny green and the dark brown bark cracks into thin, squarish plates.

Midland Hawthorn, *Crataegus laevigata*, is a rare deciduous tree, native to Britain and Europe, from which most of the commonly planted cultivated forms are derived. *Crataegus laevigata* cv. 'Paul's Scarlet' has beautiful, red, double flowers. *Crataegus laevigata* cv. 'Plena' has white double flowers that become pink as they mature.

Above *Sessile Oak:* below *English Oak photographed 27 September*

Oak at Pooley Bridge, Cumbria

English Oak

Quercus robur is a deciduous tree, native to Britain, Europe, east Russia, south-east Asia and North Africa, renowned for its longevity (possibly over 800 years old) and its valuable timber. In open ground it develops broad, spreading branches, making the overall tree wider than its height, although where there is less space the tree grows taller. Its height often reaches 30–37 metres. The male catkins open in May and the cupped acorns ripen in October. The bright green leaves, tinged with brownish-red, are lobed and the brown-grey bark is deeply fissured.

Sessile Oak, *Quercus petraea*, is a deciduous tree, native to Britain, Europe and west Asia, which is very similar to *Quercus robur*. The main difference is that the leaves are distinctly stalked and the female flowers and acorns are stalkless.

Downy Oak photographed 27 September

Downy Oak in southern France

Downy Oak

Quercus pubescens is a deciduous tree, native to southern Europe, west Asia and the Caucasus. It loves a warm, light climate and siliceous or limestone soils; in these conditions it grows very rapidly. The true species is very rare in cultivation and is not planted as an ornamental. It is easily recognised by the fact that its winter buds and new shoots are covered in down and this, together with its downy leaves, has given rise to its common name.

Its height is normally 17–20 metres and it flowers at the end of May. The acorns are enclosed in tiny cups and fall in October. The lobed leaves are downy all over when young but during the summer the upper surface becomes smooth and hairless. The bark is more deeply furrowed than that of the common oak.

Above *Lucombe Oak*; below *Turkey Oak photographed 27 September*

Lucombe Oak at Kew

Turkey Oak

Quercus cerris is a deciduous tree, native to southern and central Europe as far as Turkey, which was introduced into Britain in about 1735. It has since become naturalised and is commonly grown as an ornamental in parks and gardens. Its height reaches to 40 metres. The flowers open in May and the acorns, which fall in October, have big woolly cups. The toothed or lobed leaves vary considerably in shape but are covered all over with down. The rough, grey-brown bark has streaks of orange in its deep fissures.

Lucombe Oak, *Quercus × hispanica*, is a natural hybrid between the Turkey Oak and Cork Oak. It is semi-deciduous and in winter the leaves partly turn brown but they do not fall until the new leaves appear the following spring. It can also be recognised by its spreading, upswept branches and fairly dense foliage.

Above *Red Oak*; below *Scarlet Oak photographed 27 September*

Autumnal Oaks in Upper New York State, USA

Scarlet Oak

Quercus coccinea is a deciduous tree, native to eastern North America, which was introduced into Britain at the end of the 17th century and is now frequently planted in parks and gardens because of its wonderful autumn colour. Its height reaches 25 metres. The flowers open in April or May with the new leaves, and the round acorns, half enclosed in a deep, thin-edged cup, ripen in October. The shiny green lobed leaves turn red in autumn, unless there is a severe frost. The mature, dark-grey bark has warts and fissures.

Red Oak, *Quercus rubra*, is a deciduous tree, also native to eastern North America, which is the best growing American oak in Europe. It is often confused with the Scarlet Oak but has larger, less lobed, duller green leaves which turn yellow then deep red and finally brown in autumn. The longer, more shallow cupped acorns take two seasons to mature.

Above *Holm Oak;* below *Cork Oak photographed 27 September*

Holm Oaks at Kew

Holm Oak

Quercus ilex is a broad, evergreen tree with dense, wide-spreading foliage, native to the Mediterranean region, and commonly planted for ornament or shelter in Britain. Its height reaches 28 metres. The male and female catkins open in May or June when the new leaves appear and the acorns fall in October. The young leaves are downy but as they mature the upper surface becomes dark glossy green. The black bark cracks into small squares.

Cork Oak, *Quercus suber*, is an evergreen tree, native to the western Mediterranean, which is found in collections in Britain. In Spain and Portugal the thick, corky bark is stripped from the tree every ten years to provide most of the world's cork. Its height can reach 20 metres. The flowers open at the end of May and the short-stalked acorns fall in October. The underside of the dark, glossy leaves are covered in grey down.

Maidenhair Tree photographed 13 October

Maidenhair Tree at Kew

Maidenhair Tree

Ginkgo biloba is a deciduous tree, native to China, which was introduced into Britain in 1758 and is commonly found in parks and gardens, particularly on chalk or limestone soils in the south and west. It is the only surviving species of a group of plants that was common in prehistoric times. The unusual shape of its leaves makes it one of the most distinctive and beautiful of trees.

Its height is normally about 30 metres. The male and female flowers are produced on separate trees and open in March. The fruit only appears after good summers and develops into an edible nut surrounded by a fleshy layer that becomes smelly and slimy as it decays. The grey, brown or pale orange bark becomes ridged and fissured on mature trees.

Tulip Tree at Kew

Tulip Tree photographed 18 June

Tulip Tree

Liriodendron tulipifera is a deciduous tree, native to eastern North America, which was introduced into Britain by 1688, although probably before, and is now planted as an ornamental in parks and gardens. This tall, stately tree has a domed crown, wide-spreading branches and a thick columnar trunk. In North America the smooth, yellowy, fine-grained timber is known as 'white wood' and is used widely for house interiors because it does not split easily. The bark has a pleasant, pungent smell and a heart stimulant has been extracted from it.

Its height can reach 45–58 metres in the wild and some specimens in Britain have reached over 30 metres. The tulip-shaped flowers open in June and July and the fruit ripens from green to brown in September. The large, wide, 4-lobed leaves turn a rich yellow and orange in autumn.

Sweet Gum photographed 14 July

Sweet Gum at Wisley

Sweet Gum

Liquidambar styraciflua is a deciduous tree, native to the eastern United States and Central America, which was first introduced into Britain in the 17th century and cultivated in gardens and parks on account of its fine foliage and slender pyramidal head. Its timber is often called 'satin walnut' and is used in furniture making. It is sometimes mistaken for a maple because in autumn its leaves turn to beautiful shades of purple, crimson and orange but it is distinguishable from all maples by its alternate leaves.

Its height reaches 45 metres in the wild but in cultivation it is only about half that size. Its male and female flowers open in May and the dark, purplish-brown fruits develop in a roundish cluster. The wide, 5- or 7-lobed leaves, with finely-toothed edges are glossy above with rust-coloured tufts on the vein axils beneath.

London Plane photographed 2 May

London Planes in a London square

London Plane

Platanus acerifolia is a deciduous tree which is now thought to be a hybrid between *Platanus orientalis* and *Platanus occidentalis* although no one is certain as to when and where this cross-pollination took place. However, some of the largest existing trees are well over 200 years old. Seemingly immune to polluted air and restricted root space, the London Plane flourishes in city parks, streets and squares throughout southern England and central Europe.

Its height reaches over 30 metres. The male and female flowers, in separate, round clusters, open in May, turn brown in autumn and disperse towards the end of winter, often blocking gutters. The lobed, toothed leaves can be very variable in size and shape, even on the same tree; they colour orange and yellow in autumn. The brownish bark peels off in patches exposing lighter, smoother bark beneath and creating a mottled effect.

Norway Maple on Deeside, Aberdeenshire

Norway Maple photographed 14 July

Norway Maple

Acer platanoides is a deciduous tree, native to Europe southwards from Norway, which was introduced into Britain many centuries ago and can now commonly be found planted for ornament or shelter in streets, parks and large gardens. One of its characteristics is that it bursts into blossom in spring, before the leaves appear.

Its height normally reaches about 20–27 metres. The bright, greeny-yellow flowers appear in clusters at the end of March and the nearly horizontal, winged fruits ripen from green to brown and often remain on the tree throughout winter. The stems of the finely-pointed, 5-lobed leaves exude a milky sap if broken and the foliage turns beautiful shades of yellow, orange and red in autumn.

Sycamore photographed 14 July

Sycamore near Brechin, Angus

Sycamore

Acer pseudoplatanus is a deciduous tree, native to central and southern Europe, which was introduced into Britain at some unknown date in the Middle Ages. Sycamore is a very hardy tree, grown in streets and parks throughout Britain and sometimes cultivated as a coastal shelter tree because it can withstand strong salt-winds. It is also much planted for its smooth, strong, creamy wood which is used in making furniture and musical instruments.

Its height normally reaches 30 metres. The pendulous, greeny-yellow flower clusters open in April. The sharply-angled, winged seeds often turn red during the summer and fall in autumn. The large, shallow-toothed leaves have either 3 or 5 lobes and sometimes red or pinky-yellow stems. The metallic grey bark is smooth until tough plates fall away exposing fresh, light brown bark below.

Sugar Maple in Upper New York State, USA

left *Sugar Maple;* right *Silver Maple photographed 14 July*

Sugar Maple

Acer saccharum is a deciduous tree, native to eastern North America, which is sometimes grown for ornament or shade. It is famous for its sap and its beautiful autumn foliage. Its height reaches 30–36 metres. The long-stalked flower clusters open in April and the seeds are winged. The veined, 5-lobed leaves are downy on the under surface.

Silver Maple, *Acer saccharinum*, is a deciduous tree, native to eastern North America, which has been successfully planted for ornament in parks, gardens and on roadsides. Its height reaches to 36 metres. Its bright, yellowy-green flowers open in March before the leaves, and the stalked fruits have twisted, angled wings. The shiny-green, 5-lobed leaves are silvery underneath and turn red and yellow in autumn. The smooth grey bark is often covered with suckers.

Field Maple photographed 14 July

Field Maple in Westonbirt, Gloucestershire photographed 14 July

Field Maple

Acer campestre is a deciduous tree, native to Britain, Europe, the Near East and North Africa, which is commonly found along hedgerows and waysides. Our only native maple, this pretty, round-headed tree favours limy soils so is found most often in the south and east.

Its height normally reaches 5–10 metres although it can reach 26 metres. The numerous, greeny-yellow flower clusters open in May and are cross-pollinated by bees. They then develop into horizontally-winged fruits which eventually get blown away by the wind, lie dormant for 18 months until a warm spring day, and then germinate on waste land. The grey-green leaves, on long stalks that exude milky sap, have 3 or 5 irregular-shaped, veined lobes which turn gold or red in autumn. The rough, fissured, grey-brown bark divides into squares.

Italian Maple

Italian Maple

Italian Maple
Acer opalus is a deciduous tree, native to southern and central Europe, which was introduced into Britain in 1752 and is grown in large parks, gardens and collections for ornament. Slender, with a rounded crown and some pendulous lower branches, this pretty tree is renowned for its early flowering. It produces a spectacular display of bright yellow blossoms in March or April.

Its height normally reaches between 9–19 metres although it may sometimes be smaller and more shrub-like. Its numerous yellow flowers, each on a long hanging stalk, open in March. The downward-curving, winged fruits are pinky-green and the seeds turn bright red when ripe. The irregularly-toothed, shiny, dark-green leaves have 3 deeply-cut lobes or 5 shallow lobes; the undersides are paler green and somewhat downy.

Common Fig photographed 26 August

Common Fig in Chelsea, London

Common Fig

Ficus carica is a deciduous tree, native to the eastern Mediterranean and west Asia, which has been planted in Britain for centuries. It has also long been cultivated in southern Europe, and more recently California, for its wonderful, sweet fruits. Generally speaking, the climate in Britain is not warm enough for the cultivation of the fig tree primarily for its fruit.

Its height can reach 9 metres but it is often smaller and rather bushy. In May the male and female flowers develop, on separate trees, inside a pear-shaped receptacle that grows into the fruit when fig wasps pollinate them by climbing into a tiny hole at the top. The plump, succulent, pear-shaped fruit varies from green to brown to purple in colour and usually ripens in October. The 3- or 5-lobed, toothed leaves are rough and hairy on both surfaces and heart-shaped at the base.

Above *Common Horse Chestnut;* below *Red Horse Chestnut photographed 10 October*

Common Horse Chestnut

Common Horse Chestnut

Aesculus hippocastanum is a deciduous tree, native to northern Greece and Albania, which was introduced into Britain early in the 17th century and has long been planted as an ornamental, both here and in Europe, in parks, gardens and streets. With its rounded, wide-spreading crown and sticky buds that open into striking flower clusters, this is a very handsome and stately tree. The tree is beloved by children who gather the nuts and thread them on strings to play conkers ('conqueror').

Its height reaches 30 metres or more. The tall white flower-spikes open in May and the spiky, green-husked fruits split in October to reveal one or two shiny, brown conkers. The leaves have 5 to 7 irregularly-toothed leaflets which turn from emerald to dark green. The reddish or grey-brown bark splits into large plates.

Red Horse Chestnut, *Aesculus × carnea*, has red flowers, darker leaves and smooth-husked fruits.

Box Elder photographed 20 June

Variegated Box Elder near Godalming, Surrey

Box Elder or Ash-leaved Maple

Acer negundo is a deciduous tree, native to North America, which was introduced into Britain in 1688 and is now commonly planted for ornament in parks, gardens and streets. It has a wide-spreading head of branches and is inclined to lean as it matures.

Its height normally reaches to 12–15 metres. The dense, red-tasselled male flowers and the drooping, green clusters of female flowers are produced on separate trees and open in March or April. The winged fruits form acutely angled keys which ripen early, turn brown and remain on the trees after the leaves have fallen. The long-stalked leaves have 3 or 5 leaflets which are long, coarsely toothed and arranged like an ash. They turn yellow or brown in autumn and fall early. The smooth, grey-brown bark has shallow cracks and is often green with algae.

Above *Mountain Ash*; below *Service Tree* photographed 4 September

Mountain Ash

Rowan or Mountain Ash

Sorbus aucuparia is a deciduous tree, native to Britain, Europe, North Africa and Asia Minor, which is common in streets, parks and gardens. Its height reaches 15–18 metres. The creamy-white flower clusters open in May and the fruit ripens to bright red in September. The leaves have 6 or 7 pairs of leaflets which are pointed and sharply toothed except at their bases. The smooth, shiny, grey-brown bark has tiny lenticels.

Service Tree, *Sorbus domestica*, is a deciduous tree, native to southern Europe, North Africa and West Asia. Its height reaches 15–18 metres. Its creamy flower clusters open in May and the small, pear-shaped fruits are brown or red-tinged when ripe. The leaves have 11–21 leaflets and the dark brown and orange bark is broken into small plates.

Common Ash near Wye, Kent

Common Ash

Fraxinus excelsior is a deciduous tree, native to Britain, Europe and the Caucasus, which is one of our most valuable timber trees. A tall, upstanding tree with wide-spreading branches and a rounded crown, it likes a rich, moist soil and is famous for its winged seeds or 'keys' which are so-named because their shape is similar to the old-fashioned keys used for opening chests or doors.

Its height reaches from 30–42 metres. The male and female flower clusters open in April and the fruits or 'keys' turn brown in October and remain on the tree until after the leaves have fallen. The leaves have between 7 and 13 leaflets which are slender, pointed and toothed and they turn clear yellow in the autumn. The smooth, pale grey bark becomes ridged and fissured as the tree matures.

Flowering Ash at Kew

Flowering Ash photographed 18 May

Flowering Ash

Fraxinus ornus is a deciduous tree, native to southern Europe and Asia Minor, which has been cultivated in Britain since the 18th century or before and is commonly planted for ornament in parks, gardens and, sometimes, along roads. It has a dense, rounded dome of branches and very luxuriant foliage and although the blossoms have a faintly unpleasant smell they are very pretty in flower. The stems exude a sweet sap from which manna sugar is made.

Its height reaches 15–20 metres. The fragrant, whitish flowers with showy petals open, in profusion, in May, and the narrow fruits are green, turning brown just before the leaves fall. The leaves have 5–9 shallow-toothed leaflets which are long and tapered, and are smooth, dull green on the upper surface with brown or white down along the veins underneath. The dark grey to black bark is very smooth.

Walnut photographed 12 October

Walnut in southern France

Walnut

Juglans regia is a deciduous tree, the native origins of which are uncertain as it was introduced into Britain, Europe and parts of Asia, many centuries ago. It is common in the south and west of England and is highly prized for its timber, which is used in furniture making, and for the edible fruits which can either be eaten raw or pickled.

Its height reaches 23–30 metres. The yellowy-green male and female catkins open in late May or June and the smooth, round, dark green fruits ripen during the summer. The alternate leaves usually have 5 or 7 leaflets and turn from an orange-brown colour at the beginning of summer to a bright green by mid-summer. The smooth, pale grey bark has deep, wide cracks.

False Acacia photographed 24 May

False Acacia in southern France

False Acacia, Robinia or Black Locust

Robinia pseudoacacia is a deciduous tree, native to the south-eastern states of North America, which was introduced into Britain in the early 17th century and is now commonly found in city streets and parks. It produces suckers so plentifully that it has become naturalised in south-western Europe and its fine, feathery foliage and profuse blossoms make it an attractive ornamental. However, as it matures its older branches are inclined to split from the main trunk or be blown off by the wind. *Robinia* is easily identified by the paired spines at the base of each leaf.

Its height reaches to 25 metres. The fragrant, white flower clusters open in June, and the hard, bent fruit pods contain black kidney-shaped beans. The long leaves have 5–11 pairs of rounded leaflets. The dark brown bark is ridged and deeply furrowed.

Tree of Heaven photographed 14 September

Tree of Heaven at Kew

Tree of Heaven

Ailanthus altissima is a deciduous tree, native to northern China, which was introduced into Britain in 1751 and is now commonly planted as an ornamental in squares, streets and parks, particularly in the south and east. A hardy tree with strongly ascending branches forming a tall, irregular dome, it thrives particularly well in cities.

Its height reaches to 20 metres and occasionally 30 metres. The male and female flowers open in late July on separate trees. The winged fruits, produced on the female trees, ripen during August and September and consist of reddish-brown, twisted keys which are borne in huge bunches. The leaves, composed of 15–30 leaflets, can sometimes be 1 metre long on healthy, young trees. The smooth, dark grey bark is roughened and patterned with lighter streaks.

Chinese Cedar photographed 12 August

Chinese Cedar at Kew

Chinese Cedar

Cedrela sinensis is a deciduous tree, native to China, which was introduced into Britain in 1862 and is now planted occasionally in some collections and large gardens. A gaunt, open tree with a few stout branches, it is said to thrive best in calcareous soils. The young shoots and leaves have a similar taste to onions and the Chinese boil and eat them as a vegetable.

Its height reaches to 21 metres in its native habitat but so far it has only reached about two-thirds of this in Britain. The fragrant, whitish flower clusters open in June and the fruit capsule has winged seeds. The leaves have 5–12 pairs of short-stalked leaflets and are 50cm or longer. The dark pinky-grey bark of mature trees is coarsely shaggy.

Pride of India photographed 14 September

Pride of India in the Chelsea Physic Garden, London

Pride of India or Golden Rain Tree

Koelreuteria paniculata is a deciduous tree, native to China, Korea and Japan, which was introduced into Britain in 1763 and is cultivated for ornament in large gardens and collections, mainly in the south and east. The ascending, twisted branches form a wide dome on this hardy tree which likes rich, loamy soil. It is not a long-lived tree and is inclined to be attacked by coral-spot fungus.

Its height reaches from 9–18 metres. The yellow flower clusters open in August and are succeeded by pinky-red, three-sided, papery fruit capsules containing three black, pea-sized seeds. The long leaves have 9–15 irregularly-toothed leaflets which are downy underneath, dark green in maturity and yellow in the autumn. The rough, purply-brown bark has short, narrow, orange fissures.

157

INDEX

Roger Phillips has pioneered the photography of natural history which ensures reliable identification. By placing each specimen against a plain background he is able to show details that would otherwise have been lost if it had been photographed solely *in situ*. Such is the success of his technique that his books, which include the definitive guide to *Mushrooms* and *Wild Food*, have sold over a million copies worldwide. He is also the winner of numerous awards, including three for best produced and best designed books and the André Simon prize for 1983 for *Wild Food*.

Jacqui Hurst studied photography at Gloucestershire College of Art & Design, worked as an assistant to Roger Phillips for 4 years, and is now a freelance journalist and photographer, specialising in country matters.

Nicky Foy did an English degree at Queen Mary College, before training to be a teacher. After completing a one-year post-graduate degree she taught English for seven years and was Head of the Sixth Form at an inner London comprehensive. In 1982 she left teaching to become a freelance writer, researcher and editor.

Acknowledgements
We should like to thank John White of the Forestry Commission at Westonbirt Arboretum, and Malcolm Scott of Bedgebury Pinetum, Kent, and Jim Keesing of the Royal Botanical Gardens, Kew for their help and Mr & Mrs R. A. and W. L. Banks for the cones of rare conifers from Hergest Croft, Herefordshire.

First published in Great Britain 1986
by Elm Tree Books/Hamish Hamilton Ltd
Garden House 57-59 Long Acre London WC2E 9JZ

Cover design by Pat Doyle

British Library Cataloguing in Publication Data

Phillips, Roger, *1932–*
   Trees.
   1. Trees – Identification
   I. Title   II. Foy, Nicky   III. Hurst, Jacqui
   582.16   QK477.2.I4
   ISBN 0-241-11810-7
   ISBN 0-241-11758-5 Pbk

Typeset by Rowland Phototypesetting Ltd, Bury St Edmunds, Suffolk
Printed and bound in Italy by
Arnoldo Mondadori Editore, Verona